RESUMES
Made Easy

Patty Marler   Jan Bailey Mattia

Printed on recyclable paper

VGM Career Horizons
a division of *NTC Publishing Group*
Lincolnwood, Illinois USA

Library of Congress Cataloging-in-Publication Data

Mattia, Jan Bailey.
    Resumes made easy / by Jan Bailey Mattia, Patty Marler.
        p.   cm.
    ISBN 0–8442–4348–5 (s)
    1. Résumés (Employment).   I. Marler, Patty.   II. Title.
HF5383.M32   1995
650.14—dc20   95–773
                                               CIP

Published by VGM Career Horizons, a division of NTC Publishing Group
4255 West Touhy Avenue
Lincolnwood (Chicago), Illinois 60646–1975, U.S.A.

5 6 7 8 9 0 VP 9 8 7 6 5 4 3 2 1

Contents

INTRODUCTION   vi

Special Features   1

CHAPTER 1: RESUMES   2

Focusing Your Resume   2

Skills Identification   3

     List 'em   4

     Group 'em   7

     Dynamize 'em   8

     Choose 'em   12

     Order 'em   12

Work History   13

Education   15

Volunteer Experience   16

Personal Addition   17

References   18

     Include 'em   18

     List 'em   19

     Check 'em   20

     Write 'em   21

Letters of Reference   22
Optional Information   22
Putting It All Together   23
Checking It Over   24
The Completed Work   25
Feedback   25
Sample Resumes   26

CHAPTER 2: COVER LETTERS   77

The Greeting   77
Opening Sentence   78
The Content   79
The Sell   80
The Close   81

CHAPTER 3: JOB APPLICATIONS   82

CHAPTER 4: OTHER
MARKETING IDEAS   84

Sales Brochures   84
Business Cards   84

CHAPTER 5: THE NEXT STAGES   85

     Networking   85
     Job Interviews   86

THAT WAS THEN . . .   87

THIS IS NOW . . .   88

CONCLUSION   89

Introduction

Locating and securing employment in a tight job market can be difficult and frustrating. With 200 to 300 people applying for each advertised position, it is easy to see why having a dynamite resume is essential!

Resumes Made Easy starts you on the road to a successful job search. You will learn how to develop marketing tools which make you stand out in a crowd, and make you the person the employer wants to see!

Resumes launches your efforts by clearly and concisely guiding you through the process of creating a resume. Various resume options are outlined, and when you have finished the worksheets you'll have a resume that not only describes who you are, but is eye–catching and impressive as well.

"Success is sweet, but usually it has the scent of sweat about it."

George Burns

Cover Letters are the next necessary tool, and we guide you through creating letters which have impact, say something about you, and are direct and to the point.

Job Applications shows you how to best complete application forms so that you stand out.

The Next Stages gives you a brief look at what lies ahead once you have designed and completed your marketing tools.

What has changed in the resume world is reviewed in the *That was Then . . . This is Now . . .* section of the book.

Take a deep breath and jump in, we are about to begin the process of *Resumes Made Easy!*

Special Features

Special elements throughout this book will help you pick out key points and apply your new knowledge.

 Notes clarify text with concise explanations.

 Helpful Hints make you stand out in the crowd of job seekers.

 Expansion Exercises make your performance more polished.

 Horror Stories are true tales about things you will want to avoid.

 Special Thoughts will inspire and motivate you.

 ETA (Estimated Time of Achievement) Clocks outline the time it will take to create your resume and cover letter.

Good luck . . . and have fun!

Resumes

Your resume is an essential tool for your job search. An effective resume tells employers about the skills and experience you have that make you the ideal candidate for the job. It's your primary selling tool, so make it as thorough as possible. Always sell yourself. This is no time to be modest—employers assume you are outlining all your skills and qualifications in your resume.

"It is more important to know where you are going than to get there quickly. Do not mistake activity for achievement."

Mabel Newcomber

A resume is a reflection of you, and there are many options to consider. It is important your resume say something about you as an individual in addition to including all necessary skills information. There is no absolutely correct way to compile a resume, so don't be afraid to be creative and make your resume stand out.

Focusing Your Resume

Resumes should be customized for a specific type of work, so it is not unusual to have more than one. Although you may be looking for work in one general field, each company values some skills over others. For example, you may be looking for work as a teacher. You might have one resume that highlights your leadership skills, another stressing your experience with special needs groups, another emphasizing your experience teaching English as a second language.

Develop a job objective for each position you apply for. **Do not** include it, simply use it to help you stay focused when creating your resume.

Most careers are broad enough that the duties vary from company to company. Be sure to highlight the strengths you have that correspond with the primary duties you would be performing for a particular employer. As a result, you should have several variations of your resume.

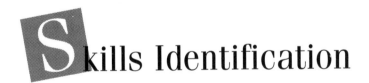

Skills Identification

"If you love what you do, you will never work another day in your life!"

Dr. Robert Anthony, *Think On*

Identifying and highlighting your skills is the most important step in creating your resume. You need to outline your skills **completely** and in enough detail for employers to get a good picture of who you are and what you have to offer. Leaving things unsaid so you have something to talk about during the interview is **not** a good idea. You will not get an interview if your resume does not say anything. Be sure to pat yourself on the back as much as possible. If you don't, who will??

Write ten positive things that happen to you each day. This may mean anything from making a positive contact at a company, to a friendly chat with the woman next door, to a great interview. You will be surprised how quickly your daily outlook will change.

ETA
1–2 hrs

List 'Em

Identify and acknowledge **all** your skills. **Do not** be humble when doing this.

1. List or tell a friend all your skills and duties from your past work and volunteer experience. Review past job descriptions, if available, to refresh your memory. Write down everything breaking your past jobs into skills.

Example:

"I was a carpenter" is too general. This may mean you were responsible for taking measurements, attending to detail, ordering supplies, supervising apprentices, interacting with customers, enforcing safety standards, projecting costs, and making coffee for the crew.

"Everyone needs long–range goals if for no other reason than to keep from being frustrated by short–range failures."

**Bits & Pieces,
January 1990**

Be specific and include all duties no matter how insignificant you think they may be. **Do not** edit at this point.

2. List **all** your personal qualities, characteristics, and skills. We often have difficulty giving ourselves credit for things we are good at, so ask the opinion of friends, family members and past co–workers.

Example:

Enjoy working with children, creative, patient when listening to friends' problems, etc.

If you have limited work and volunteer experience, this exercise is especially important. You will highlight personal skills in your resume.

You may also use this information to write your Personal Addition.

SKILL I.D.

_____
_____
_____
_____
_____
_____
_____
_____
_____
_____
_____
_____
_____
_____

SKILL HEADINGS

_____
_____
_____
_____

PERSONAL CHARACTERISTICS

_____
_____
_____
_____
_____

ETA
30 min

Group 'Em

To make your skills more easily identifiable for potential employers, you need to categorize them under general headings. Review your skill statements and decide on headings that fit your skills and are relevant to the work you are applying for. Your skills should group nicely in two to four categories.

Example:

If you are applying for retail sales positions, your headings might be:

- Communication/Interpersonal Skills
- Sales and Marketing Skills
- Supervisory Skills
- Creative Abilities and Window Dressing Skills

 Different occupations will require different skill headings. Some possible headings are:

accounting	interpersonal	program development
book keeping	laboratory procedures	promotions
budgeting	managing	reception
child care	marketing	sales
communication	mechanical	special skills
computer experience	office management	supervisory
counseling	office support	teaching
creative abilities	organization	teamwork
customer service	plumbing	technical
design	presentation	warehousing
electrical	problem solving	
instructing		

Practice telling people what you are good at. Tell yourself in the mirror and work into telling other people. With practice, this will make it much easier to sell yourself in an interview.

Remember, these are only suggestions. Use headings that apply to your own experiences.

You may create a special heading for statements of particular importance.

Example:

- Personal/Career Accomplishments
- Special Achievements
- Awards and Accomplishments
- Highlights of Qualifications

ETA
30—90 min

Dynamize 'Em

Beginning with your first statement and working through all of them, re—word or explain each skill, using clear, concise, and energetic words. You may find that during this process you combine skill statements. You might not develop a statement for each skill you have identified, but can highlight the skill later in the work history section of your resume.

Dynamize all statements under one heading before moving to the next. Some of the skills may be similar or repeated. Dynamize them only once.

How?

1. Begin statements with strong action words.

Example:

accessed
adapted
addressed
administered
advertised
advised
analyzed
applied
appraised
arranged
assessed
assigned
assumed
author
calculated
categorized
challenged
communicated
completed
conducted
constructed
consulted
cooperated
coordinated
counselled
created
defined
demonstrated
designed
developed
directed
discovered
documented
earned
edited
eliminated
encouraged

enforced
ensured
established
evaluated
exemplified
expanded
expedited
facilitated
focused
fostered
gained
generated
identified
implemented
improved
increased
influenced
informed
initiated
innovative
inspected
inspired
instructed
interacted
introduced
investigated
lectured
liaised
lobbied
maintained
managed
mediated
merged
monitored
motivated
negotiated
operated

organized
outstanding ability
participated
performed
pioneered
planned
possess
presented
produced
projected
promoted
proposed
proven ability
provided
re–aligned
recommended
re–defined
reorganized
reported
researched
reviewed
revised
scheduled
selected
self motivated
serviced
skilled
streamlined
structured
submitted
substantiated
suggested
supervised
supplemented
supported
trained
volunteered

2. Highlight skills with strong descriptive words.

Example:

confidently	extensively
consistently	positively
continually	productively
cooperatively	professionally
creatively	proficiently
diplomatically	quickly
eagerly	sensitively
effectively	sincerely
efficiently	skilfully
energetically	substantially
excellent	successfully

**While reading a resume I was feeling quite low,
For there were words used that I didn't know.
So I looked up the list,
And found they didn't exist!
To the garbage that one did go!**

3. State the skill clearly, indicating how or where you used it.

4. Convert all statements to past tense.

Example:

From: Type reports.

To: Accurately typed and edited monthly and annual reports.

Notice the skill is clarified when you describe the type of reports. The statement has energy and impact because it emphasizes how you completed the reports—accurately.

From: Supervise staff.

To: Monitored productivity, assigned tasks, and appraised performance of eight staff members.

Notice the difference. Which person sounds more competent?

Dynamize 'Em

Choose 'Em

You may have more skills under one heading than another. On average, three to seven descriptive phrases for each heading is appropriate.

If you have less than three, ask yourself if the heading is really necessary?

Yes?   Develop additional phrases.

No?   Delete the heading and redistribute phrases.

Do everything possible to leave on good terms with your employer and co–workers. Every city is a small one.

If you have more than seven, can you re–organize?

Yes?   Choose an additional heading and divide the phrases accordingly.

No?   Delete or combine statements unrelated to positions you are applying for.

Order 'Em

Employers work under time restrictions and may only skim phrases, so your strongest statements must appear first. A strong initial statement encourages employers to continue reading.

"The difference between a successful career and a mediocre one sometimes consists of leaving about four or five things unsaid."

***Bits & Pieces*, January 1990**

Example:

Consider how re–ordering the following skills ensures that the most important ones stand out.

From:

- Work well individually and as a team member.

- Maintain confidentiality and discretion in handling situations

- Negotiated union and non–union agreements using common sense, good judgement, sincerity, and realistic budget considerations.

- Effectively responded to a wide range of employee concerns regarding benefit packages.

To:

- Negotiated union and non–union agreements using common sense, good judgement, sincerity, and realistic budget considerations.

- Effectively responded to a wide range of employee concerns regarding benefit packages.

- Maintain confidentiality and discretion in handling situations

- Work well individually and as a team member.

ETA
30 min

ork History

List in *reverse* chronological order all your jobs from the past 15 years. Use **accurate** dates (by year and month), company names and job titles.

You may also wish to include a brief description of your job duties under each position or specific accomplishment in your work history section.

Example:

October 1990 – November 1993
Accounting Manager
JPS Accounting Inc.

March 1987 – July 1990
Accountant
Johnny Red's Bar and Grill

You may have difficulties describing your work history, but there is always a solution.

Problem: No paid work history.

Solution: Elaborate upon your volunteer experience, education and unpaid work experience. Your resume may not contain a Work History component, or it may consist of unpaid work. (i.e., if you are a recent graduate or homemaker)

Problem: Absent from the work force for several years.

Solution: Record, with dates, your relevant activities during that time. (i.e. primary care–giver, household manager, re–training, sabbatical, travelling)

**There once was a man who
   did barter,
We're hoping he's now become
   smarter,
He said if given a chance,
He'd teach us all to dance
What would he trade if he'd
   been made a partner?**

Problem: Sporadic work history or numerous gaps.

Solution: Record the years you worked rather than the months.

**Be prepared to answer questions about
work history gaps in an interview.**

ducation

Including an Education section is a personal choice. You may have a solid educational background related to the job you are applying for, or your related education may be limited. If a position requires a specified educational background, make sure to include an Education section. Record, as you did in *Work History*, your *Education History*.

 Document the education most relevant to your job objective, followed by other education.

Example:

1976–1980	Bachelor of Commerce Degree Business University Localcity, Here
1968–1970	General Accounting Diploma Business College Bigcity, Foreigncountry
1982–1990	Various Accounting Courses Various Locations

Consider:

You may choose not to include the following if you feel it may limit your opportunity for employment.

1. The dates you received your education.

2. The location you received your education.

3. Education unrelated to the work you are applying for.

ETA
15 min

Volunteer Experience

Include all volunteer activities, beginning with those most relevant to your job objective. You may or may not choose to include dates.

Example:

Treasurer for local community league
Coach for Little League baseball and soccer
Canvasser for Heart and Stroke Foundation

WORK HISTORY

_____
_____
_____
_____
_____
_____
_____
_____

VOLUNTEER EXPERIENCE

_____
_____
_____

EDUCATION

_____
_____
_____
_____
_____

Personal Addition

Highlight, in paragraph format, the reasons an employer should hire you by illustrating your strong personal and/or work–related characteristics. You may include personal interests, activities, or hobbies in this section.

ETA
30 min

"It takes as much courage to have tried and failed as it does to have tried and succeeded."

Anne Morrow Lindbergh

Your personal addition may replace a cover letter for some resume styles, so be sure your personality and character is reflected.

Example:

1. I am a dedicated and detail–oriented person committed to safe and accurate research. I understand the need for ongoing commitment to products like those developed by reputable organizations, and find great reward in being part of that development. Please know that I love the work that I do and the opportunity it provides to help people.

2. Customer service is the key to the success of any sales person and my proven sales record illustrates perfectly my positive and genuine approach to customer service. As a veteran salesperson, I am well–versed in the techniques needed to stay on top of any market. With increased market competition, "working smart" is essential. I enjoy the dynamic environment of sales and look forward to being a productive team member.

Consider your job search a job itself. Maintain your schedule and dress appropriately when you leave the house.

3. Upon researching your organization, I discovered our views for the future are very much aligned. Computerization is the wave of the future and your company is on the leading edge. I, too, excel in the computer industry. I have all the latest technology on my system at home and routinely design my own programs to meet changing needs. I find the prospect of working for a progressive company such as yours very exciting and am certain I would be a productive member of your team.

 See sample resumes for additional examples.

ETA
30 min

eferences

Include 'Em?
· ·

Employers prefer you do not fold your resume in letter–size envelopes or encase them in plastic.

Should you choose not to include your references with your resume, be sure to present them during interviews.

Some employers consider a resume incomplete if references are not included. It is possible that you would be excluded from a competition if you do not include them. However, should a potential employer call a reference prior to short–listing candidates, and the reference given is simply "OK," you may also be eliminated. The choice is yours to include them or not.

List 'Em

Create a list of individuals who would present you positively to a prospective employer, preferably those who can discuss your work habits. Your list might include:

> Supervisors
> Co–workers
> Volunteer coordinators

 "Life's what's *coming* not what *was*."

Dr. Robert Anthony, *'Think On'*

Three work–related references is ideal. If you have only one or two, include a character/personal reference section, which might refer a potential employer to:

> Teachers
> Doctors
> Other professionals

Do not include family members or relatives.

Check 'Em

**There was a man who we
 once would have hired,
We called references and about
 him inquired.
Imagine our dread,
When we learned they were dead!
From their companies they'd
 certainly retired!**

1. Call each reference and ask for permission **prior** to giving a potential employer their name. Be sure to ask if they will give you a **positive** reference. If they will, verify their current employer, title, and phone number.

2. Have a friend call to verify the reference is indeed a good one. Be prepared by having a 'job' in mind that you are applying for (one that fits your skills) and a list of questions to ask.

Example:

1. What were *Pat's* work habits: punctuality, days missed, initiative, dependability, etc?

2. Did *Pat* work well with others? Independently?

3. Was *Pat* productive, accurate, and thorough?

4. Was *Pat* able to resolve problems independently?

5. Did *Pat* work well with customers?

6. Was *Pat* effective under pressure?

7. Given that chance, would you hire *Pat* again?

If the reference did not convince your friend to hire you, it will not convince an employer either. Look for another reference!

Write 'Em

Write down the references you will use.

 If your reference has changed jobs, include their current title, company and phone number, in addition to the company where you were employed together.

Example:

Joe Knowsme
Office Manager
XYZ Corporation
Formerly: Office Supervisor, PastCo.
(123) 555–1212

 Whenever possible, drop off your resume in person and ask if there is someone available to speak to.

PERSONAL ADDITION

_____

_____

_____

_____

REFERENCES

_____

_____

_____

_____

ETA
15 min

Letters of Reference

Attach positive letters of reference to your resume. If you have several, choose the three best ones which are most related to the job you are applying for and attach these. Even if employers say they do not require reference letters, they leave a good impression.

ETA
15 min

Optional Information

Include additional sections in your resume if the information would provide insight to your character and is pertinent to your job objective.

Example:

Associations and Affiliations
Awards and Acknowledgements
Interests and Activities
Areas of Expertise
Special Qualifications
Future Goals

Avoid the use of florescent paper. While catchy at first, it soon becomes hard to read.

Putting It All Together

Choose the material you will include in each resume. Remember, you will probably have more than one resume. Tailor each resume so the information included is relevant to the particular position you are applying for.

You have the content of your resume. Now, you must choose the presentation. There are many options, and how you personalize your resume is up to you.

"Kind words can be short and easy to speak, but their echoes are truly endless."

Mother Theresa

DO NOT limit yourself to what you feel is **normal**, **standard**, or **expected**! Your resume is a reflection of you. Employers quickly tire of looking at 200 copies of the same resume style, so make sure yours is **DIFFERENT** AND **INTERESTING**!!

How?

Consider EVERYTHING!

Paper Quality: Believe it or not, the feel of the paper is important. Buy good quality resume stationary.

Paper Colour: Subtle colours are best.

Print Quality: Use a new printer ribbon. There is nothing worse than straining to see the print on the paper. A resume that's hard to read will end up in the garbage!

Print Style: Funky and interesting is great, but can you read it?

Layout:	Be creative! Don't think you need to do what everyone else does!
Spacing:	Leave spaces on your resume to give the reader's eyes a break!

 Above all else, do not be afraid to be you. If that means using graphics or doing something you have never seen before, try it. It might turn out better than you thought!

ETA
30 min

hecking It Over

When you feel your resume is complete and virtually employer–ready, have someone else proofread it.

Have them look for:

your **correct** address and phone number

spelling errors

capitalization problems

past tense consistency

aligned text

grammatical errors

consistent punctuation, i.e. periods throughout

spacing: is it easy to read?
is it nice to look at?

Does it make sense? Does it say what you want it to say? Does it have an impact?

Ask your friend to provide as much feedback as possible. The extra work you do now will pay off in the long run.

ETA
30–90 min

The Completed Work

A professional–looking resume **must** be done on a computer or type-writer. A computer and laser printer are preferable.

If you do not have a computer, there are many locations where you can rent one and have a laser print made of your resume. It will pay off!

Feedback

After you have submitted your resume, ask the employers for feedback. They may be uncomfortable providing this information, so it is up to you to phrase your questions in such a way that the employer can comfortably answer.

How?

- Tell the employer your resume is new and ask for their comments, impressions, and suggestions.

- If you were not chosen for an interview, ask what qualifications, education, and experience the job candidates have.

- If the employer still refuses to provide feedback, thank them for their time anyway. Leaving your meeting on a positive note will leave the door open for future contact.

Sample Resumes

The following pages contain many sample resumes. Look at them not only for ideas on *what* to put in your resume, but also *how* to put things together.

Remember, the first step is to get an employer to look at your resume. The second step is to keep them interested! Do not be afraid to try your own ideas.

Linda Stevenson
3928 – 31 Street
Toronto, ON
T6T 1J6
(416) 555–3283 (h)
(416) 555–4794 (w)

Personal Addition

I enjoy a challenging work environment and get along well with co–workers. I am focused and disciplined, with a strong work ethic, and adapt quickly to a continually changing work atmosphere.

I am a quick learner, and know my ability to develop rapport with others and my open communication style would make me a valuable asset to your team.

Relevant Skills and Experience

Child Case Management

- Develop and promote positive relationships and activities with children.

- Responsible for the successful community reintegration of case load, including: education, work, and family or foster care.

- Design and implement daily living schedules and organize activities for facility residents.

- Screen and assess clients prior to development of personal treatment programs.

- Investigated reports of fraudulent Provincial Family and Social Services claims.

- Gained a practical working knowledge of Young Offender, Child Welfare, National Evidence and Narcotics Control Act, Charter of Rights and City Bylaw Legislation with City Police Service.

- Possess a genuine concern for the development and well being of clients.

Communication and Interpersonal

- Provide daily structure and counselling for dysfunctional youth.
- Broad knowledge of and experience working with various cultural and age groups.
- Creative and innovative team member.
- Travelled to client residents to interview them regarding benefits.
- Effectively managed potentially volatile situations.
- Quickly develop excellent rapport with others.

Organizational and Managerial

- Perform Social Service intake duties to determine client eligibility.
- Developed and implemented employee training programs.
- Documented client interactions and prepared computer graphs, weekly estimations, and progress reports.
- Reported findings and made recommendations to appropriate authorities.

Education

Sept. 1992 – Present	**Social Work Diploma Program**
Sept. 1989 – 1991	**Law Enforcement Diploma Program**
	City College

Related Course Work

Child Abuse Prevention	Family Violence and Crisis
Understanding Suicide Prevention	Sexual Assault and Sexual Abuse
Peer Conflict Mediation	Child Self Esteem
Leadership and Development	National Coaching Certification
KOGA Arrest and Control Tactics	Fetal Alcohol Syndrome Seminar
St. John Ambulance First Aid	

Linda Stevenson
(416)555–3238 (h)
(416)555–4794 (w)

Volunteer Experience

- *City Police Service: Sex Crimes and Child Abuse Unit*
  Investigated child abuse and neglect cases.
- *Seventh Step Society: City Institution*
  Participated in group meetings helping inmates modify criminal behavior and attitudes.
- *Warren House*
  Attended crisis intervention training seminars. Worked effectively supporting women and their children in crisis situations.
- *Catholic Social Services: Child Treatment Program*
  Helped emotionally disturbed children understand their feelings and modify behavior to function productively in the community.
- *Youth Emergency Shelter: Volunteer Youth Worker*
  Acted as a positive role model for youth. Participated in group activities and disciplined destructive behavior.
- *Spearhead Youth Centre*
  Worked with dysfunctional youths, attempting to reintegrate them into society.
- *Boys and Girls Club*
  Encouraged children to develop positive relations with staff, peers and family, in addition to developing their own self–worth.
- *Big Sisters and Big Brothers Society*
  Supported a young Native American girl from a dysfunctional family, encouraging her independence.

Employment History

Nov. 1992 – Present	Brocop Homes: Front Line Child Care Worker
Jan. 1992 – July 1992	Triple Dean Corporation: Security Officer
Oct. 1991 – Feb. 1992	Seventh Step Society: Volunteer Counsellor
June 1991 – Oct. 1991	City Family and Social Services: Fraud Inspector
April 1990 – June 1991	Youth Emergency Shelter: Volunteer Youth Worker
Sept. 1990 – Dec. 1990	City Police Service: Telephone Survey Supervisor
April 1990 – Sept. 1990	City Police Service: S.T.E.P. Student Placement
April 1990 – Aug. 1990	Safety Patrol Dog Services: Security Officer

Linda Stevenson
(416)555–3238 (h)
(416)555–4794 (w)

References

Pam Moffat
Case Load Worker
Big Sisters and Big Brothers Society
(403) 555–8181

Brian Aldson
Residential Manager
Brocop Homes
(403) 555–4794

Eldon Fry
Instructor
Law Enforcement Program
City College
(403) 555–5656

Linda Stevenson
(416)555–3238 (h)
(416)555–4794 (w)

Dennis MacLeod

898 Sunset Drive
Alameda, New Mexico 57678
(222) 555–8293

HIGHLIGHTS

- 20 years experience in the dry cleaning industry.
- Owned and successfully managed dry cleaning and restaurant businesses.
- People–oriented: Relate well to and enjoy meeting and working with people.
- Self–motivated, possessing the ability to recognize and resolve problems.

WORK EXPERIENCE

Aug. 1994 – Present	Subcontractor, Roadrunner Messenger Service Alameda, New Mexico
March 1994 – June 1994	Production Manager, Spot Out Cleaning Albuquerque, New Mexico
Sept. 1991 – Feb. 1994	Subcontractor, Roadrunner Messenger Service Alameda, New Mexico
March 1991 – Sept. 1991	Supervisor, No 1 Cleaners Albuquerque, New Mexico
Nov. 1986 – Dec. 1990	Owner/Manager, Dennis's Pizza Albuquerque, New Mexico
April 1985 – Aug. 1986	Subcontractor, We Deliver Messengers Albuquerque, New Mexico
Dec. 1973 – Feb. 1985	Owner/Manager, Professional Cleaners Alameda, New Mexico

**Experienced
Self–motivated
Ambitious
Responsible**

Dennis MacLeod

(222) 555–8293

EXPERIENCE AND SKILLS

Management

- Trained staff to serve customers promptly and courteously, handle complaints effectively, and complete drycleaning duties.
- Completed long–term and short–term financial planning, and tended to accounts receivable, accounts payable, daily sales reports, banking, cost control and inventory.
- Developed marketing and promotion strategies.
- Involved in community activities with business; sponsored sports teams and participated in trade fairs.
- Interviewed, hired, supervised, disciplined, and laid off staff.
- Key player in team management decisions.
- Monitored production and supply cost levels.

Teamwork

- Mediated disagreements and encouraged open and honest communication.
- Maintained a calm and professional attitude when dealing with staff and customers.
- Motivated staff to work hard and take pride in their job.
- Developed a positive rapport with customers to build a repeat clientelle.

Technical

- Completed all drycleaning functions: cleaning, spotting, pressing, etc.
- Designed layout of drycleaning business.
- Conducted routine equipment maintenance checks, scheduled repairs, then ensured machines were in proper running order.
- Experimented with different suppliers and products to achieve the highest quality results.
- Discovered long–term problems in established businesses and resolved them promptly.

Organization

- Stayed up–to–date on government regulations regarding hazardous waste and product management.
- Organized staff and workload schedules and ensured work was completed and distributed to various worksites on time.
- Assumed responsibility for ordering supplies and maintaining cleanliness of stores.
- Implemented and maintained strict quality standards.

Yvonne Bradley – Mariner
Brentwood Crescent
Springfield, Missouri 54365

CARING

Patient, understanding, and loving and believe these qualities are essential to working effectively with children.

COMMITTED

Dedicated to developing curriculum which stimulates children and encourages creative thought and play.

EXPERIENCED

Eight years experience developing children's programs, monitoring children's development and working and playing with children.

(222) 555–2490

WORK EXPERIENCE

June 1993 – Present
Private Child Care
Springfield, Missouri
Provided home day care service which met the needs and strengths of individual children

January – June 1993
Primary Caregiver
Cared for my own child

Nov 1991 – Nov 1992 & April 1989 – Feb 1990
Child Care Worker
Rainbow Street Child Care Center
Springfield, Missouri
Developed programs and monitored progress of children attending the centre

May – June 1992
Private Nanny
Preston, Missouri
Cared for children and took care of household responsibilities

Dec 1988 – June 1991
Supervisor/Waitress
Nevada's Seafood Restaurant
Preston, Missouri
Supervised staff and completed general waitress duties

Oct 1986 – Dec 1987
Supervisor/Cashier
K–Mart
Springfield, Missouri
Supervised staff and attended to customers as a cashier

Jan 1986 – Dec 1987
Child Care Worker
City of Springfield, Missouri
Organized and set up activities for children

June 1986 – Dec 1987
Mobile Playground and Park Information Attendant
City of Springfield, Missouri

RELEVANT SKILLS AND EXPERIENCE

CHILD CARE

- Set up appropriate activities for children indoors and outside; cooking, painting, crafts, reading books, etc.
- Monitored gross motor, fine motor, social, language and cognitive development
- Organized multicultural special events
- Observed and recorded the development of each child
- Administered first aid and medication when required
- Assumed parental responsibilities when minding children
- Bought and supplied meals for children
- Maintained cleanliness throughout centre and in individual homes

PROGRAM DEVELOPMENT

- Identified children's needs and developed appropriate programs
- Organized special outings for children
- Planned and organized daily activities considering children's needs and strengths
- Liaised with community organizations to set up field trips
- Advertised children's program by developing posters and letters to parents
- Advocated for children and maintained high program standards

Yvonne Bradley–Mariner
(222) 555–2490

SUPERVISORY AND COMMUNICATION SKILLS

- Trained and supervised staff
- Discussed problems and monitored staff performance
- Communicated director's concerns to room staff and vice versa
- Gave and received positive criticism
- Recognized when conflicts arose and effectively resolved them
- Communicated effectively with staff, children, and parents
- Ensured safety standards were met
- Organized staff rosters and breaks, opened and closed centre
- Balanced daily child care payments and made bank deposits

EDUCATION

Associate Diploma in Social Science of Child Studies
1990 – 1991
St. Louis Technical College
St. Louis, Missouri

High School Diploma
1984 – 1986
Springfield Composite High School
Springfield, Missouri

PERSONAL ADDITION

I feel I would be an asset to your organization as I am enthusiastic, energetic and outgoing. I am hard–working and willing to do shiftwork and have done it in the past. I am a people person and enjoy working and communicating with children, fellow employees, and surrounding people.

REFERENCES AVAILABLE ON REQUEST

Relevant Skills and Experience

Communication and Interpersonal

- Supervised staff; consistently maintained a positive work attitude.
- Trained new personnel, ensuring continued customer service.
- Work effectively individually and as a team member.
- Maintain a positive and professional attitude dealing with customers.
- Professional and courteous approach to customer service.
- Excellent Public Relations skills; work well with diverse groups of people.
- Diplomatic and tactful with professionals at all corporate levels.
- Excellent oral and written communication skills.
- Confident public speaker, enjoy presenting new information to customers.

Organizational and Managerial

- Outstanding ability to initiate action, make decisions and solve problems.
- Highly motivated to accept responsibility and work without supervision.
- Open to learning, adapt well to challenging and continually changing situations.
- Successfully prioritize daily routine.
- Proven ability to set and meet deadlines.
- Continually upgrading skills and qualifications.
- Well-organized, energetic, and dependable; can be counted on to see projects through to completion.
- Proven ability to anticipate client needs and ensure customer satisfaction should problems arise.
- Poised, confident, and productive under pressure.

Ann Marie MacLeod

#36, Pine Avenue
Decatur, IL
92038

(123) 555–3283

References

Carl McBride
Banquet Manager
Westward Inn
Decatur, IL
(123) 555–7770

Joan Chappley
Owner
Steve's Restaurant
Decatur, IL
(123) 555–3390

Darryl Pickar
Dining Room
Manager
Westward Inn
Decatur, IL
(123) 555–7770

Ann Marie MacLeod

(123) 555–3283

Personal Addition

I enjoy a dynamic work environment and get along well with co–workers. I am focused, disciplined, and assertive and have a strong work ethic. My experience is diverse and I excel in situations where customer service is essential.

I am a team player and work hard to ensure customer needs are met quickly and efficiently. With my skills and experience, I am sure I would make a positive addition to your organization.

Employment History

1993 – Present   Service Staff
Steve's Restaurant, Decatur, IL
- Developed excellent communication, problem–solving, and time–management skills.
- Effectively manage dissatisfied customers, ensuring continued patronage.

1987 – 1993   Supervisor, Bartender, Cashier, Service Staff
Westward Inn, Decatur, IL
- Trained new personnel, ensuring continued customer service.
- Ordered and maintained sufficient bar inventory.
- Responsible for accurate management of cash flow.

1990 – 1991   Personnel Administrator; Receptionist/Secretary
Professional Personnel, Decatur, IL
- Interviewed applicants as potential placement staff.
- Administered all necessary tests to determine placement eligibility: typing, math, and spelling tests and Wonderlic personality assessment.
- Assisted in management of office accounting: payables/receivables, invoicing, and payroll.
- Maintained office supply inventory.

1986 – 1987   Security Guard
Airtight Security Services, Decatur, IL
- Involved in providing security for temporary workers during postal strike.
- Monitored computerized alarm systems for office towers.
- Liaised with police service during emergency situations.
- Responsible for hourly security reports.

Ann Marie MacLeod

(123) 555–3283

Education and Additional Courses

1991 – Present	Social Work Diploma McNally Community College (part–time)
1993	English Writing & Communication Certificate City Vocational College
1992	Building Self–Esteem for Children
1990	Effective Telephone Communication Certificate
1985 – 1986	Educational Upgrading, City College

Volunteer Experience

1990 – Present Big Sisters and Big Brothers Society of Decatur
- Provide a positive role model for Little Sister from a dysfunctional family environment.
- Support and counsel family members to improve family dynamics.

1992 Seven Steps Society
- Counselled and rehabilitated offenders.
- Assumed an active role in promoting the positive reintegration of offenders into society.

ALLAN ARNOLD
Box 1896
Glasgow, Montana

555–4464

PROFESSIONAL STRENGTHS AND HIGHLIGHTS

Extensive managerial experience within Montana Grain Co–Op area operations

Efficient management of staffing and grain and agricultural sales

Excellent communication skills

MANAGEMENT/ORGANIZATIONAL EXPERIENCE

Administered human resource functions: hiring, evaluation, compensation, discipline and termination

Monitored area operations, identified problems and provided solutions to assure day–to–day operations were productive

Efficiently administered operating budgets

Planned efficient utilization of staff and product in order to give quality customer service

Ensured accurate and efficient operation of grain elevator

Stayed abreast of Montana Grain Co–Op policies, procedures, and goals

Monitored competition

Monitored upkeep and maintenance of facilities and equipment

COMMUNICATION SKILLS

Provided effective two–way communication between staff, management and delegates

Facilitated resolution of misunderstanding between customers, staff, and management

Promoted Montana Grain Co–Op products

Acted as a liaison with staff, regional office, community agencies, farm organizations, and railways

EMPLOYMENT HISTORY

UNIT MANAGER: MONTANA GRAIN CO–OP 1991 – Present

Responsible for efficient and accurate operation of unit
Coordinated and administered 'On–Target' operating budgets

AREA MANAGER: MONTANA GRAIN CO–OP 1988 – 1991

Developed annual capital and operating budgets
Administered efficient utilization of human resources
Maintained a positive work environment for employees

TRAVELLING SUPERINTENDENT: MONTANA GRAIN CO–OP 1984 – 1988

Supervised 52 staff members (including 21 Elevator Managers)
Coordinated and administered human resource issues
Implemented cost–efficient methods to maintain and replace facilities and equipment

STATION MANAGER 1969 – 1984

Managed day–to–day activities of grain elevator: receiving, storing and shipping of grain
Marketed agricultural products

EDUCATION

DIPLOMA IN AGRICULTURE
Lloyd Prince's Agricultural College

HIGH SCHOOL DIPLOMA
Scobey Composite High School

AWARDS AND ACHIEVEMENTS
TOP ACHIEVER AWARD: 1988–1989 AND 1989–1990
PERFORMANCE AWARD: 1987–1988
SERVED ON TECHNICAL TASK FORCE

ALLAN ARNOLD
555–4464

JOHN T. BRADY

12238–104 Street
Jacksonvillle, Florida 97234
USA
(602) 555–9253

Personal Overview

I enjoy a challenging work environment and get along well with co–workers. I am focused and disciplined with a strong work ethic, and adapt quickly to a continually changing work atmosphere.

Working in the education field has allowed me to pursue my commitment to lifelong learning. I have a curiosity of other lifestyles, cultures and world issues and enjoy the diversity of cultures and attitudes that teaching affords me.

I am a quick learner and know my ability to develop rapport with others and my open communication style would make me a valuable asset to your team.

Relevant Skills and Experience

Instruction and Facilitation

- Facilitate curriculum in a self–paced learning environment to first, second, and third year apprentices: lab, theory and code.

- Develop supplementary material for courses, including exam modification and learning module revision.

- Design and develop demonstration boards for practical electrical labs.

- Instruct English as a second language to students requiring English in a trade environment, in conjunction with the Adult Vocational College.

- Facilitate National Electrical Code courses with the Continuing Education division of NAIT.

- Advise and counsel students regarding their progress throughout the duration of their NAIT training.

- Technical Education advisor to students from Foreign Countries visiting NAIT for technical upgrading:
  - Advise regarding most beneficial curriculum choices,
  - Tutor students with specific needs,
  - Introduce students to Western Culture.

Electrical

- Designed and developed a training program for the Sign Installer Association:
  - Researched industry ensuring relevance of information,
  - Developed print ready self–paced modules.

- Provided Commercial installations including welders, cranes, motors and lathes.
- Completed all aspects of residential wiring.
- Foreman for commercial installations ranging from 1000 to 20,000 square feet.
- Coordinated large commercial projects: ordered materials, ensured quality and timely job progression.
- Provided electrical maintenance for the greater Metro area, including fire alarms, magnetic starters, three phase motors, power and lighting circuits.
- Oilfield maintenance electrician: wired explosion proof lights and heaters, maintained motors and generators.

Computer

- Proficient in the use of: Microsoft Word, SuperPaint, WordPerfect and DOS.
- Completed print ready electrical drawings in SuperPaint.
- Designed and formatted an entire modular training package for student use, using Microsoft Word and SuperPaint.
- Skilled in the use of Campus America, the NAIT modular computer system.

Education

1987 – 1991	Bachelor of Education (Vocational) University of Iowa Minor: Social Studies
1981 – 1986	Florida State Technologies Journeyman Electrical Certificate

Additional Courses

Electricity I	Alan–Bradley 217 Programmable
Electricity II	Logic Controller (PLC)
Electricity III	Alan–Bradley SLC 100 (PLC)
DC Generators	Smart House Installation
Fire and Alarm Systems	H2S Safety Alive Program

JOHN T. BRADY
(602) 555–4290 (H)
(602) 555–7044 (W)
(602) 555–7402 (FAX)

Employment History

August 1991 – Present Instructor, Electrician Program
Florida State Technologies
- Instruct Electrical Apprentices in addition to developing curriculum.

August 1991 – Present Owner/Operator
Double T Technologies
- Electrical installation and maintenance.

1989 – 1990 Journeyman Electrician
Action Electric
- Foreman for Electrical Installations.
Involved in city–wide maintenance.

1988 – 1989 Journeyman Maintenance
Electrician
Clearing System
Incorporated (CSI)
- Maintenance electrician in the oil field industry.

1986 – 1987 Journeyman Electrician
Ed's Electrical Services
- Electrical installations for commercial and residential properties.

References

Jan Simbal
F S T Electrician Program
Program Head
(602) 555–7055

Marley Glenn
Action Electric
Owner/Operator
(602) 555–3440

Larry Singh
Clearing System
Incorporated
Owner
(602) 555–5132

JOHN T. BRADY
12238–104 STREET
JACKSONVILLLE, FL 97234
USA

(602) 555–4290 (H)
(602) 555–7044 (W)
(602) 555–7402 (FAX)

Sindy M. Howe
13 Aldergrove, Regina, SK
S4M 5B7
555–1265

Relevant Skills and Experience

Case Load Management

- Effectively liaised between foster homes and government and private agencies to provide aid for children and teens.
- Performed home visits to determine appropriate counselling and support needs for families.
- Select, train support and monitor dayhome providers ensuring quality child care.
- Assessed client needs, assisted in development of case plans, monitored client progress.
- Facilitated positive relations between support home staff and resident teens.
- Offered crisis intervention to families escaping abusive situations.

Communication and Interpersonal

- Facilitated workshops for day home providers: child abuse, family violence, and nutrition for children.
- Proven ability to quickly develop trust and excellent rapport with clients.
- Sensitive to issues and concerns of lower income, Native American, and dysfunctional families.
- Maintain a positive and professional attitude dealing with clients.
- Helped children and teens develop positive self–concept and self–esteem.

Organizational and Managerial

- Monitor 35 day homes, providing government documentation, assessment, and progress reports.
- Maintained a licensed facility for 80 children; trained and supervised 20 staff, performed payroll and budgeting duties, enforced regulations and standards.
- Well–organized and can be counted on to prioritize and see projects through to completion.
- Plan and implement workshops for day home providers.

Education

1993	Social Work Diploma Olive MacLelan Community College
1991	Early Childhood Development Diploma Olive MacLelan Community College
1990 – Present	Bachelor of Social Work University Faculty of Extension *completed 2 of 4 years*

Employment and Work Practicum Experience

July 1993 – Present	**Day Home Consultant** Norwood Family Day Home Agency, Regina, SK

- Assess, select, train, support and monitor day home providers.
- Maintain concise and accurate records and progress reports to submit to supervising government agency.
- Consistently monitor day homes to ensure standards of quality child care are being met.

October 1993 – Present

Relief Youthworker
Delaney House, Regina, SK

- Assess and provide support, guidance, and constructive activities for teens in the house.
- Act as a positive role model for dysfunctional teens.

September 1992 – April 1993

Case Worker (Work Practicum)
Family and Social Services, Regina, SK

- Worked as a member of a Temporary Guardianship Order team working progressively toward counselling and uniting dysfunctional families.
- Assessed clients and families, helped develop action plans, and monitored progress through home visits.

May 1992 – August 1992

Child Support Worker
Support Shelter Society, Regina, SK

- Provided crisis intervention for mothers and children; developed programs and activities for children; provided essential resources and support for mothers.

September 1991 – April 1992

Assistant Case Load Worker (Work Practicum)
Macleod Youth Services, Regina, SK

- Liaised between government and private agencies, gaining necessary support and treatment for clients.
- Facilitated positive relations between workers and teens.
- Designed and implemented daily living schedules and activities for facility residents.

May 1991 – August 1991

Child Support Worker
Support Shelter Society, Regina, SK

- Helped develop and foster children's sense of self–worth and self–esteem.

Sindy M. Howe

January 1991 – April 1991	**Child Care Worker (Work Practicum)** Norwood Community Center, Regina, SK

- Offered support and referrals for food, clothing, and other life essentials for inner– city families.

September 1990 – December 1990	**Child Support Worker (Work Practicum)** Support Shelter Society, A Safe Place, Edmonton, AB

- Supported and provided appropriate agency referrals for mothers and children escaping abusive situations.

July 1990 – August 1990	**Childcare Worker (Work Practicum)** Feldman Childcare Society, Regina, SK

- Developed and implemented age appropriate activities for children aged 2 to 3 years.

September 1981 – December 1989	**Director** D&B Childcare Center, Regina, SK

- Maintained a licensed facility for 80 children: hired and trained 20 staff.
- Developed and implemented age–appropriate activities.
- Performed all administrative duties: payroll, budgeting, enforcing regulations.

Volunteer Experience

February 1994 – Present	**Distress Line Worker** The Safety Net

- Provide support and immediate resource referral to callers.

October 1990 – January 1993	**Childcare Worker** Support Shelter Society, Regina, SK

- Provide assistance and resources to mothers and children leaving abusive homes.

Additional Course Work

Family Dynamic, Olive MacLelan Community College

Adolescent Issues, Case Management, Group Counselling, Distress Line Training Program, The Safety Net Support Shelter, Volunteer Training

First Aid, Child CPR, St. John's Ambulance

References

Helen Ricardo
Director
Support Shelter Society
555–7233

Lenora Mikasco
T.G.O. Unit Supervisor
Family and Social Services
555–6725

Jeanine Yarmuck
Assistant Coordinator
Norwood Family Day Home Agency
555–1301

Debra Delaney
Director
Acadia House
555–5511

Brian Davey

Box 4678
Ft. Worth, TX
98365

(123) 555–5065 (h)
(123) 555–6214 (w)

Employment History

July 1990 –   Senior Warehouseman
Present   State Power Limited
                   Distribution & Service Centre

- Fully conversant with all aspects of computerized inventory and control management system including Bar Code.
- Certified, safe forklift operator: narrow aisle and counter balance.
- Extensive experience with substation electrical components, transmission, and distribution hardware.
- Safety Chairman January 1993 to January 1994

September 1989 –   Generation Labourer
July 1990   State Power Limited
                   Isolated Projects Division

- Installed and maintained diesel power plants throughout Northern Texas.

September 1988 –   Warehouseman
September 1989   State Power Limited
                   Engineering & Construction
                   Warehouse

- Quickly and efficiently filled orders.
- Maintained neat, safe, and efficient work environment.

October 1987 –   Floor Supervisor/Bar Manager
August 1988   Clyde's Restaurants Limited

- Hired and trained staff.
- Supervised and ensured efficient and courteous service of restaurant customers.

April 1986 –   Apprentice Lineman
December 1986   State Power Limited

- Constructed and maintained distribution and transmission lines.

Brian Davey

(123) 555–5065 (h)
(123) 555–6214 (w)

Employment History Continued

October 1983 – April 1986	Warehouse Foreman EZ Electric Supplies Limited

- Supervision of employees and efficient completion of warehouse duties.

August 1982 – December 1982	Survey Aide (seasonal work) State Forestry, Lands and Wildlife

October 1979 – April 1982	Survey Aide State Transportation

Relevant Skills and Experience

Warehousing and Organizational

- Efficiently perform inventory duties including: maintaining computerized records, cycle counting program, preparing shipments and restocking inventory.
- Certified counter balance and narrow aisle forklift operator.
- Responsible for assisting in reorganization of warehouse after relocation.
- Successfully prioritize daily routine.
- Knowledgeable in the operation of State Power inventory control system: MMS and OPS.
- Continually upgrading skills and qualifications.
- Skilled in the operation of material handling equipment.
- Well–organized and can be counted on to see projects through to completion.

Brian Davey

(123) 555–5065 (h)
(123) 555–6214 (w)

Communication and Interpersonal

- Supervised staff; consistently maintained a positive work environment.
- Hired and trained new personnel ensuring continued customer service.
- Work effectively individually and as a team member.
- Knowledgeable in the use of DOS and WordPerfect for Windows.
- Professional and courteous approach to customer service.
- Communicate well with a wide variety of people.
- Enjoy assisting clients and sales representatives with their concerns.

Education and Additional Courses

1994	Introductory Computer Course: DOS and WordPerfect for Windows
1993	International Material Management Level 3
1992	International Material Management Level 2
1990	International Material Management Level 1
1983	TECH Pre–Technology Program: including Math, English and Physics

References Available Upon Request

Aaron Dalemont

134 Greenwood Way
Billings, Montana
90372, USA
555–4839

⌐ Special Achievements

- Committed and dedicated to ensuring time schedules and deadlines are met.
- Supervised crews of tradesmen: 15 – 30 production operators.
- Experienced in budgeting and managing projects in a cost effective manner.

Relevant Skills and Experience

⌐ Supervisory Skills

- Hired and maintained a staff of qualified operators to perform tasks within safe production guidelines.
- Conscientiously ensured and maintained above–average safety standards.
- Excellent foreman: developed a strong working relationship with co–workers and employees, promoting efficient completion of work.
- Monitored and evaluated employee performance and implemented an operator rotation system to increase productivity.

⌐ Organizational Skills

- Effective trouble–shooter: assessed situations and made decisions to prevent problems.
- Performed regular machinery checks to ensure the efficient working of equipment.
- Efficiently monitored and adjusted costs to keep projects operating within budget constraints.
- Proven ability to meet deadlines.
- Created and developed appropriate forms for documentation.

Aaron Dalemont

555–4839

⌐ Employment History

1990 – Present   General Manager
Deep Wood Logging
(Contract Position)

- Coordinated and managed entire project: hired qualified staff, purchased equipment, and evaluated overall progress within budget constraints.
- Responsible for recruiting and training a suitable employee from the area to assume the management role of the project for the maintenance stages of the project.
- Ensured all environmental regulations were met and often surpassed in daily workings of the company.

1962 – 1990   Independent Logging Contractor
(Various Employers)

- Began as a manual logger and upgraded over the years, becoming fully experienced with mechanical logging.
- Owned and contracted equipment and an experienced labour force for a variety of logging jobs.
- Constantly evolved with the times, learning new methods and techniques, updating equipment, and always maintaining respect for the environment.

⌐ Volunteer Experience

- Weekend relief worker, CityWide Animal Shelter
- Volunteer Crisis Worker, Suicide Hot–line

References Available upon Request

Roy Scheaffer
1443 – 57 Street
Dallas, TX
94756
(123) 555–1265

Employment History

June 1992 – Present **Shop Foreman**
Bargain Heating
Dallas, TX

- Coordinate residential and commercial projects: price quotes for customers and material ordering
- Supervise apprentice sheet metal mechanics
- Maintain safe and efficient working environment

June 1989 – **Journeyman Shop**
May 1992 **Apprentice**
Bargain Heating
Dallas, TX

- Fabricated for residential and commercial heating and ventilation projects
- Fabricated kitchen exhaust dust collection projects
- Experienced welder: MIG, Carbon, Arc and TIG
- Skilled fabricator for various custom projects

December 1988 – **Apprentice Sheet**
June 1989 **Metal Mechanic**
(Field Worker)
NorState Metal Fabricators Inc.

- Efficient field installation of industrial projects

December 1987 – **Apprentice Sheet**
December 1988 **Metal Mechanic**
Ten Gallon Industries Ltd.
Dallas, TX

- Installation of multiple story building heating and ventilation systems: worked on City Centre Project

1982 – 1987   Sheet Metal Mechanic

- Worked as a union sheet metal mechanic on varied projects

Education

1993   Journeyman Sheet Metal Certification

- Including Interstate Red Seal
- TTI (Texas Technology Institute)

High School Diploma
City Vocational College

Personal Addition

Proven ability to work within time restrictions

Maintain strong leadership skills working toward a common goal

Work well individually and as a team member

Energetic and hard–working

Enjoy golf, hockey, softball, and spending time with family

References

Mark McNab
Manager
Bargain Heating
555–3741

Cody Muldoon
Estimator
Airway Heating Ltd.
555–0491

Ian Kilroy
Journeyman Sheet Metal
Mechanic
Airway Heating Ltd.
555–0491

Personal Reference

Bernard Klaus
Operator
Link Petroleum
555–6574

Roy Scheaffer
(123) 555–1265

Tammy Scott

123 Adia Boulevard
Salinas, California 54980
555–9571

EMPLOYMENT HISTORY

November 1990 –   Insurance Telephone Adjuster,
Present   Crown Insurance

- Efficiently investigated, negotiated, and settled property and automobile claims.
- Conducted automobile claims training sessions.
- Focused on settling claims and issuing payments to injured clients.
- Professionally and calmly handled stressful situations.

March 1989 –   Claims Clerical Personnel,
October 1990   The Mutual Insurance Company

- Accurately received and entered data on insurance claims.
- Reviewed and settled windshield claims.
- Communicated concerns and questions on client claims.

February 1989 –   Secretary for Life Insurance Department,
August 1989   The Mutual Insurance Company

- Answered telephones and accurately advised employees of all messages.
- Carefully arranged all mail.

ABOUT ME!

The ability to work alone, retain information, and learn quickly are a few of my strong points.

I work with heavy workloads and limited time frames on a daily basis, and complete tasks with limited direction and supervision. I have worked in the insurance industry for the past five years and have developed excellent interpersonal skills and the ability to handle stress.

I love learning and am a devoted and eager employee. When working for a company I strive for excellence and promote the agency enthusiastically!

RELEVANT SKILLS AND EXPERIENCE

Communication

- Extensive working relationships with many brokers, contractors, and customers.
- Communicate ideas well on a one–to–one basis and by means of written correspondence.

Organization

- Manage high work volume on a regular basis.
- Excellent prioritizing skills.

EDUCATION

1989 – 1990	Business Administration California Insurance College
1993	"Automobile Insurance" Insurance Institute of California
1993	Stress Management Seminar
1992	Business Writing and Grammar
1992	Commissioner for Oaths
1990	"Principles and Practices" Insurance Institute of California
1988	General Diploma River View High School

Tammy Scott 555–9571

Ross Schultz

123 Seaside Road
Vancouver, B.C.
V5R 1P3
(222) 555–8678

WORK EXPERIENCE

**Sept. 1990
– Present**
Senior Service Representative
Scientific Instruments, Hope, B.C.

• Serviced and maintained medical, research, and industrial instruments.

**March 1984
– Sept. 1990**
Technical Service Representative
Scientific Instruments, Kelowna, B.C.

• Maintained and serviced laboratory instruments.

**May 1983
– June 1983
& Sept. 1983
– Jan. 1984**
Operator/Laborer
Rockstone Inc., Whistler, B.C.

• Operated portable sawmill.

• Assisted carpenter.

**July 1983
– Sept. 1983**
Fish Guide
Fishing Plus, Whistler, B.C.

• Escorted guests on fishing tours.

• Maintained boats and engines.

**June 1979
– Aug. 1979**
Mechanic's Assistant
The Marina, Squamish, B.C.

• Repaired marine, chainsaw, and lawnmower engines.

• Installed throttle, gearshift and steering controls on boats.

**Energetic
Self Motivated
Hard Working**

Ross Schultz

(222) 555–8678

RELEVANT SKILLS AND EXPERIENCE

Technical

- Serviced clinical instruments and completed scheduled maintenance calls.
- Gave technical support over the telephone.
- Determined appropriate action to be taken: if the customer could independently solve the problem, if a service call was required, or if an instrument should be sent in.
- Sourced technical information through manuals and technical bulletins.
- Provided estimates for equipment repairs.

Organization

- Prioritized service calls.
- Scheduled work at customer's convenience.
- Monitored inventory and ensured adequate stock was available. Reordered parts when stock at minimum level.
- Coordinated service calls with maintenance calls.

Teamwork

- Created positive rapport with co–workers.
- Looked for sales opportunities for the company.
- Brainstormed ways to streamline the company's operations.
- Work equally well as a team leader and player.

Communication

- Calmed excited customers so they could give required information: nature of problem, urgency, and customer's ability to complete simple repairs on their own.
- Questioned customer to see if problem was hardware, software, or application oriented.
- Provided step by step problem–solving instructions over the telephone.

Ross Schultz

(222) 555–8678

PERSONAL ADDITION

You will find that I am a very sincere person. I enjoy working hard both mentally and physically. I work well on my own and as part of a team. I take pride in my work and take great satisfaction in a job well done.

I have a great sense of humor and am people–oriented. Getting to know my customers is a part of the job I enjoy. I am always eager to learn more and improve my skills.

EDUCATION

Diploma of Technology in Electrical Technology and Instrumentation
British Columbia Institute of Technology, 1982

High School Diploma
Frank Sr. High School, 1980
Whistler, B.C.

FURTHER EDUCATION

- Programming in Fortran
- Introduction to DOS
- Programming in Basic
- St. John's First Aid Course
- WHIMIS Course

STEVEN BASIL

EDUCATION

September 1989 – April 1992 University of Florida
University Faculty: Rehabilitation Services

September 1988 – April 1989 University of
Alabama, Birmingham
Faculty: English

September 1986 – April 1988 Spring Hill College, Mobile
Alabama Faculty: General Transfer Program

EMPLOYMENT HISTORY

September 1992 – Present (half–time)

Speech Language Pathologist
Early Entry for Special Needs Program,
Gainesville, Florida

- Diagnose speech and language disorders in pre–school children with multiple disabilities, both mental and physical.

- Facilitate the development of communication skills, including oral, sign language, articulation, and switch use in a classroom based setting.

- Demonstrate early–intervention techniques and provide information to parents during home visits.

5 5 5 • 8 9 5 8

STEVEN
BASIL

EMPLOYMENT HISTORY (Continued)

September 1992 – Present

Speech Language Pathologist
Centre for Language and Learning
Gainesville, Florida

• Provide classroom–based and pull–out intervention for learning disabled teenagers.

• Work with team members to develop, implement, and revise individual goals on a continuing basis.

• Facilitate students' development of social language, memory, vocabulary, metalinguistic, and problem solving skills.

• Co–facilitate "Interactive Development of Language" class and a "Language for Social Situations" group session.

September 1991 to April 1992

Clinical Materials Room Manager
Florida State University

• Monitored materials on loan to speech pathology and audiology students.

• Assisted students in finding appropriate diagnostic and treatment materials.

May 1989 to August 1989

Day Care Worker
Gainesville, Florida

• Planned, prepared, and carried out daily care, education and recreation activities for preschool children.

5 5 5 • 8 9 5 8

STEVEN
BASIL

VOLUNTEER WORK

July 1985 to July 1986 (full time)

Day Care Worker
Friendship Day Care
Hutchinson, Kansas

• Monitored children's recreational activities.

• Implemented lesson plans and assisted pre–school children in developing self–help skills.

AFFILIATIONS AND CERTIFICATES

The Speech and Hearing Association.

The National Association of Speech Language Pathologists and Audiologists.

First Aid in Child Care Certificate.

555 • 8958

Relevant Skills and Experience

Sales and Promotions

- Strongly self–motivated, enthusiastic, and committed to financial success in sales.
- Earned employee of the month awards for outstanding sales and service.
- Excellent presentation skills; comfortable in front of various group sizes.
- Consistently achieve and maintain high sales volumes.
- Possess a genuine interest in customer service and satisfaction.
- Involved in developing restaurant promotions successfully, increasing client base.
- Sound working knowledge of IBM Word Processing programs.

Communication and Interpersonal

- Creative and innovative team member; work well individually and as a productive team player.
- Dynamic and effective communicator; excellent oral and written communication skills.
- Effectively manage potentially volatile situations, ensuring a positive outcome satisfying all parties.
- Calm, poised and productive under pressure.
- Broad knowledge of and experience working with various cultural and age groups.
- Quickly develop excellent rapport with others.

Organizational and Managerial

- Proven ability to work independently with increasing responsibility.
- Innovative, quick learner with proven ability to adapt well to change.

Bert Tieu

8133 – 32 Avenue
Phoenix, AZ
48376

(123) 555–7593

References

Mark Barcus
Manager
XXY Diagnostics
Corporation
(123) 555–3921

Lorna Hogle
Assistant Manager
The Inn
(123) 555–6415

Jim Milne
Owner/Partner
Star Consulting
Group
(123) 555–7450

Bert Tieu

---

(123) 555–7593

Communication and Interpersonal Continued

- Implemented effective training methods to increase staff efficiency.
- Maintain a positive and professional attitude at all times.
- Proven time–management skills; effectively prioritize workload.
- Organized and managed all aspects of recreational sports team.

Emplyment History

January 1988 – Present   The Inn
- Fine dining service
- Established and maintained regular clientele
- Assisted in maintaining exclusive wine inventory

June 1986 – February 1988   Chachi's
- Trained new service staff
- Recognized for outstanding sales

September 1984 – May 1986   Foodstuff's
- Maintained large produce selection

Summer 1984   National Park Lodge
- Promoted positive customer relations in dining room

Bert Tieu

———

(123) 555–7593

Education

1989	Bachelor of Science University of Wisconsin
1984	Advanced High School Diploma Arnlay Composite High School

Personal Addition

I enjoy excitement and challenge in the work place where there is a cooperative team environment. I am focused, disciplined, and self–motivated, and have a strong work ethic. Adapting well to a quickly changing work atmosphere, I excel in the necessarily dynamic field of sales.

The pharmaceutical industry is an innovative industry which is continually growing and changing. There are always new drugs being developed, giving those working in the industry the opportunity to learn about new relationships between drugs and the human body. This introduction of new drugs into the pharmaceutical market guarantees an exciting environment, one which I am certain I would excel in.

Brad Garris

401, 35 Maple Ridge Cres.
Charlotte, NC
90234

(123) 555–5065 (h)
(123) 555–6214 (w)

Personal Overview

- *Proven ability to work within time restrictions*
- *Work well individually and as a team member*
- *Always willing to take on additional tasks with increasing responsibility*
- *Maintain strong leadership skills working toward a common goal*
- *Energetic and hard–working*

Relevant Skills and Abilities

Communication and Interpersonal Skills

- *Supervised staff; consistently maintained a positive work environment*
- *Hired and trained new personnel, ensuring continued customer service*
- *Work effectively individually and as a team member*
- *Knowledgeable in the use of DOS and WordPerfect for Windows*
- *Professional and courteous approach to customer service*
- *Communicate well with a wide variety of people*
- *Enjoy assisting clients and sales representatives with their concerns*

Warehousing and Organizational Skills

- *Efficiently perform inventory duties including: maintaining computerized records, cycle counting program, preparing shipments and restocking inventory*
- *Certified counter balance and narrow aisle forklift operator*
- *Responsible for assisting in reorganization of warehouse after relocation*
- *Successfully prioritize daily routine*
- *Knowledgeable in the operation of City Power inventory control system: MMS and OPS*
- *Continually upgrading skills and qualifications*
- *Skilled in the operation of material handling equipment*
- *Well–organized and can be counted on to see projects through to completion*

_____*Brad Garris*

Employment History

July 1990 – Present
Senior Warehouseman
City Power Limited, Distribution and Service Centre
- *Safely operate material handling equipment*
- *Accurately complete computerized inventory duties*

September 1989 – July 1990
Generation Labourer
City Power Limited, Isolated Prjects Division
- *Installed and maintained diesel power plants throughout Northern Iowa*

September 1988 – September 1989
Warehouseman
City Power Limited, Engineering and Construction Warehouse
- *Quickly and efficiently filled orders*
- *Maintained neat and efficient work environment*

October 1987 – August 1988
Floor Supervisor/Bar Manager
Steve's Restaurants Ltd.
- *Hired and trained staff*
- *Supervised and ensured efficient and courteous service of restaurant customers*

April 1986 – December 1986
Apprentice Lineman
City Power Limited
- *Constructed and maintained distribution and transmission lines*

October 1983 – April 1986
Warehouse Foreman
RL Electric Supplies Ltd.
- *Supervision of employees and efficient completion of warehouse duties*

August 1982 – December 1982
Survey Aide *(seasonal work)*
Forestry, Lands and Wildlife

October 1979 – April 1982
Survey Aide
Transportation, Regional Services

Education

1994 *Introductory Computer Course: DOS and WordPerfect for Windows*

1993 *International Material Management Level 3*

1992 *International Material Management Level 2*

1990 *International Material Management Level 1*

1983 *Pre–Technology Program: including Math, English and Physics*

_____*References Available Upon Request*

Brad Garris

401, 35 Maple Ridge Cres.
Charlotte, NC
90234

(123) 555–5065 (h)
(123) 555–6214 (w)

Robert Fowler

946 Kangaroo Crescent
Alexandria 2017
Sydney, NSW
Australia
(23) 768–1053

Employment History

Nov 1988 –
March 1994

Fowler & O'Neill
Self Employed Drywaller
– Set up small business from scratch and ran it successfully for
  5 years
– Purchased materials, vehicles, and tools
– Communicated well with clients, builders and salespeople
– Carried out specific details from builders and interior designers
– Worked under deadlines and pressure
– Balanced books, distributed wages, paid bills and completed
  invoicing

Jan 1987 –
Nov 1988

North Bay Drywalling Limited
Drywall Fixer
– Involved in all aspects of drywalling: suspended ceilings, completed set-
  tings and fixings
– Worked off a plan
– Worked long hours under pressure
– Work well as a team player and able to receive constructive criticism

Jan 1986 –
Dec 1987

Hardwick Industries
Contract Supervisor
– Completed day–to–day liaison with site management of the prime con-
  tractors involving setting of schedules etc.
– Organized and set duties of manpower on two sites, i.e. recommended
  manning levels, induction, time keeping, etc.
– Organized equipment and materials as required by each site i.e. day to
  day hardware items, and deliveries.
– Submitted reports to ACI Fibreglass office as required and maintained
  site diary
– Liaison with various committees on each site to facilitate smooth operation of work program, i.e. Unions, Site Safety Committee, and various
  other trades

Feb 1982 –
Dec 1985

Alexandra Knitting Mill Limited
Driver, Maintenance, Warehouse

Work Experience Continued

Sept 1980 –
Oct 1981

Fowler & Radwick
Self Employed Carpenter
– Involved in all aspects of building houses: foundations, flooring, framing, roofing, cladding, interior linings, cleaning, and setting out
– Communicated effectively with partner and clients
– Responsible for invoicing, pricing and balancing books

Jan 1977 –
Aug 1980

Lyle May Builders
4 Year Carpentry Apprenticeship
– Apprenticed in carpentry (cottage industry)

Education

Dry Plasterers Contractors Licence
Sydney, Australia, 1988

Carpentry Apprenticeship Completed
The Poly Technical College, New Plymouth, New Zealand, 1978

Successfully Completed High School
Francis Douglas Memorial College, New Zealand, 1976

Interests

Hobbies: Stain glass windows, model toy car collector, bush walking
Sports: Rugby Union: 3 Years Club Captain
                        First grade captain

References Attached

Robert Fowler
(23) 768–1053

Karen Tomas

11324–136 St.
Portland, Oregon
43533
(123) 555–7108

Education

**Engineering Design and Drafting Technology
Diploma, 1992–1994**
Oregon Institute of Technology, Portland

Pre–Technology Accelerated Program, 1992
Oregon Institute of Technology, Portland

Licensed Hairstylist, 1984
Selecte College, Portland

Technical Skills

Municipal Drafting
- Performed calculations relating to precipitation and runoff measurements
- Designed roads, street grades, and sewer and water for small residential subdivisions
- Prepared legal surveys and right–of–way drawings

Contract Law
- Basic knowledge of the Canadian Judicial System
- Knowledge of specific contract documents
- Prepared basic specifications

Building Services
- Designed small HVAC mechanical systems
- Apply heat analysis to ducting and hot water heating designs

Photogrammetry
- Perform calculations relating to scale of aerial photographs
- Identified cultural and natural land features and geological land forms

Process Piping
- Designed API–650 storage tank with welding details and pressure vessels to American Society of Mechanical Engineers standards
- Calculated heating surface area, maximum working pressures, and hydrotest pressures
- Perform calculations relating to scales of aerial photographs

Surveying
- Prepared field notes
- Familiar with third system of surveying and working knowledge of levels and transit

Work well alone and in a group.

Able to **meet deadlines**.

Committed to working hard and developing my skills.

Dedicated to my work and the company I work for.

Karen Tomas

11324–136 St.
Portland, Oregon
43533
(123) 555–7108

Work Experience

For the past 14 years I have held various positions in the service industry.

Hairstylist (1984–1992)

Responsible for general administrative duties, providing hair services to clients, training assistants, merchandising, and completing accounts payable.

Store Clerk

OREGON LIQUOR CONTROL BOARD (1992)
OREGON LIQUOR DISTRIBUTION BRANCH (1991)

Responsible for large sums of money, re–stocking of shelves, and customer service.

Golf Proshop Attendant (seasonal 1987–1989)

Responsible for equipment rentals, registrations, handling of daily finances, bar service, maintenance and fundraising.

Volunteer Work

Student Public Relations Participant at OIT open house
Coordinated fundraiser for golf club expansion
Involved in fundraising with OIT Graduation Committee

Accomplishments and Associations

I am currently a member of AET (Association of Engineering Technologists). Throughout my employment and educational career, I have developed good organization and communication skills. I am efficient in the handling of daily finances of operations and have coordinated a fundraiser for a local golf club expansion.

References

Roy Sargent
Assistant Program Head
Engineering Design and
Drafting Technology
Oregon Institute of
Technology
w) 441–7697

Gerry Banner
Instructor
Engineering Design and
Drafting Technology
Oregon Institute of
Technology
w) 441–7604

Eileen Gould
Assistant Manager
w) 461–2815

EMPLOYMENT HISTORY

Oct. 1991 –   Instructor/Counsellor
May 1993   Independent Career Counselling Inc.
- Developed and facilitated workshops and provided individual counselling in a federal government funded project for adults over age 40
- Liaised, networked, and made referrals to various organizations and agencies

Dec. 1990 –   Research Assistant
June 1991   John Robinson Rehabilitation Hospital
                 Department of Social Work
- Researched and developed reports, protocols and technical guides
- Developed and presented information sessions and orientation videos
- Updated resource library and directories

Sept. 1988 –   Social Worker
Aug. 1990   Ontario Social Services
                 Income Support
- Issued monthly social allowance cheques, emergency vouchers and special needs money
- Effectively managed a caseload of 230 families
- Frequently performed crisis interventions

1987   Research Assistant
Summer   Services for Children Inc.

1986   Child Care Worker
Summer   Wee Child Daycare Society

1984   Instructor/Lifeguard
Summer   Rainbow Pool

PERSONAL ADDITION

Working under stressful conditions reacting cool and calmly, and taking control in emergency situations are few of my strong qualities. I have worked in demanding conditions as a Social Worker and have responded to numerous emergencies as a Lifeguard and at recreational sporting events. I am a self starter with initiative who can also take direction from others.

I have extensive telephone experience. 90% of my work as a Social Worker was completed over the telephone and my communication skills are excellent.

As a native 'Carlisle–ian, I am familiar with the one addressing system and the many services and resources available. I also have an extensive knowledge of the resources available in Toronto.

I am interested in dispatching for the Carlisle Fire Department and part-time work appeals strongly to me. I am excited about the possibility of working with your company and will call the second week of October to answer any further questions you may have.

ACCOMPLISHMENTS AND AWARDS

Sportsman – like playing for recreational slowpitch team

Most Valuable Player for Volleyball

High School Students – Union President

Honor Roll

Scholarships in High School and University

Mr. Conrors Athletic Scholarships

Justin Greene
555–5687

Resume Inside

REFERENCES

Rudy Maxwell
Coordinator
Independent Career Counseling Inc.
Toronto, ON
555–4567

Manning Earley
Program Planner
Ontario Social Services
Toronto, AB
555–9876

Bao Tsu–Lee
Manager
Hue Health Care Clinic
Formerly: Department of Social Work Supervisor
        John Robinson Rehabilitation Hospital
555–8045

JUSTIN GREENE
123 WYE ST.
CARLISLE
ONTARIO,
J8H 9K8
555–5687

J U S T I N

123 WYE ST., CARLISLE, ONTARIO J8H 9K8
555–5687

EDUCATION

1988   Bachelor of Science Degree:
          Specialization in Psychology
          University of Toronto

1991   Suicide Prevention Course

1992   Counsellor's Responsibilities and Boundaries

1984   Advanced High School Diploma
          Sarnia Composite High School

RELEVANT SKILLS & EXPERIENCE

COMMUNICATION

- Extensive experience responding to individual's needs over the telephone
- Able to calm and direct individuals in emergency situations
- Communicate ideas well in group settings and on a one to one basis
- Take charge and respond calmly in emergency situations

ORGANIZATION

- Efficiently managed high work volume on a regular basis
- Assessed individual needs and resolved problems effectively
- Excellent prioritizing skills

G R E E N E

EDUCATION

FACULTY OF NURSING, COLLABORATIVE PROGRAM
3rd Year, UCLA, 1991–1994

Faculty of Science
UCLA, 1989–1991

Advanced High School Diploma
John Stewart Composite High School, 1986–1989

EMPLOYMENT HISTORY

Sept. 1992 –   Head Coach
Present   Santa Ana Keyano Swim Club
- Head coach for Midget division of Keyano Swim Club, Winter Session

July 1992   Coach
                    UCLA Summer Sports Camp
- Coached Swimming

May – Aug   Case File Researcher, Clerk III
1990 & 1991   California Land Compensation Board
- Searched and documented case files relating to land compensation hearings and performed basic office duties

Jan 1991 –   Child Care Worker
Dec 1991   Wee Care After School Program
- Provided activities and care for children grades 1 through 6 after school

June – Aug   Head Coach
1990 & 1991   Santa Ana Keyano Swim Club
- Head coach for Midget division of Keyano Swim Club, Summer Program

7 Weeks   Coach
1990, 1991, 1992   Olympic Start: Learn to Swim Program
- Taught children ages 5 through 12 basic competitive swim skills

SARA MERLIN • (121) 555–4141

Aug 1989   Physiotherapist Assistant
                    Southside Physical Therapy Clinic
- Aided one physiotherapist with basic treatment and office duties

SKILLS AND EXPERIENCE

RESEARCH SKILLS

- Completed research papers relating to occupational therapy, the nursing process, patient assessment, needs assessment for community based programs, HIV, infant transplant and cardiac nutrition
- Currently taking a nursing research course focussing on how to analyze research papers and carry out research projects
- Reviewed Land Compensation Board hearing manuscripts and retrieved information to enter in a data base program

NURSING SKILLS

- Completed clinical rotations in the following areas: urology, orthopedics, cardiology, community health, pediatrics and obstetrics, and mental health
- Effective patient education techniques; develop innovative and interesting ways to teach patients
- Work well on multidisciplinary health care teams to increase the quality of care for patients
- Enjoy making clients comfortable in all situations
- Would like to do more work in critical care areas: emergency, intensive care, operating room, and cardiac care units

ORGANIZATIONAL SKILLS

- Excellent time management skills; coordinate and organize time effectively
- Enjoy being busy but am careful not to take on too much so as to overwhelm myself

---

- Coordinated fund raising events and graduation ceremonies for two Registered Nursing programs
- Coordinate work and time so all clients' needs are met

LEADERSHIP SKILLS

- Encourage and motivate people to perform to their highest potential
- Coached swimming for the Santa Ana Keyano Swim Club for 4 years
- Involved in Nursing Students Association and Grad 1995 council

REFERENCES

May Forester, Executive Director
Santa Ana Urban Development Board
Santa Ana, California
Formerly: Director of the California
          Land Compensation Board
w) 555–1541

Don Silver, Head Coach
Santa Ana Keyano Swim Club
Santa Ana, California
w) 555–9448

Sue Beachman, Nurse Educator
UCLA
Los Angeles, California
w) 555–4922

PERSONAL ADDITION

I feel I would be an asset to your organization as I am enthusiastic, easy to work with and outgoing.
I enjoy working with others and helping everyone work to their full potential to benefit the organization and its clients. In essence, a teamwork philosophy. I am a quick and eager learner and hard worker who takes pride in helping others.

SARA

MERLIN

19 Mark Drive
Los Angeles, CA 64875
(121) 555–4141

CARING

Understanding clients in an empathetic way as well as being a client advocate. These are essential qualities when dealing with people.

HARD WORKING

I take pride in a job well done and ensure that each task is performed swiftly and to the best of my abilities.

COMMITTED

Dedicated to the client, the organization, and my own conscience to provide quality service and care.

RELIABLE

Punctuality, dependability and trustworthiness are all strong qualities that I believe are important to any profession or obligation.

JOANNE YOUNG

Joanne Young
14 Beach Street
52472 Range Road 224
Long Island, NY
57687

(403) 922–4347

ORGANIZED

Perform tasks promptly and accurately. Dedicated to building stronger practices and take pride in a job well done.

HARD WORKING

Possess a high energy level and am eager to complete work efficiently. Learn new skills quickly.

CARING

Patient, kind and understanding. People oriented – have others interests at heart.

EXPERIENCED

10 years experience in the dental field working in various specialty practices. Enjoy being a team player.

REFERENCES

WORK REFERENCES

Donna Mc Greggor
Office Administrator
Dr. Michael Sargent, D.D.S.
Known for 10 years
(Hm) 555–9834
(Wk) 555–3486

Diane Black
Claims Adjustor
Great West Life
(Formerly Claims Adjustor for
Prudential)
Known for 30 years
(Hm) 555–3618
(Wk) 555–4345

CHARACTER REFERENCES

Simone Harding
Manager
Diversified Auto Repairs
Known for 6 years
(Wk) 555–0912

Alec Smith
Self–Employed
Known for 4 years
(Wk) 555–4596

11" x 17" Resume – fold on dotted line for 8 1/2" x 11" brochure

WORK EXPERIENCE

March 1993 – Present
CLINICAL COORDINATOR/ DENTAL ASSISTANT
DR. MICHAEL L. SARGENT, D.D.S.
LONG ISLAND, NY
- Clinical Coordinator and Dental Assistant for esthetic and restorative dentistry practice.

January 1992 – March 1993 & December 1988 – June 1989
DENTAL ASSISTANT
DR. JOHN W. GONGOS, D.D.S.
BRENTWOOD, NY
- Assisted with dentistry done under local anaesthesia.

December 1988 – June 1989
CONSULTATION ADMINISTRATOR/ DENTAL ASSISTANT
DR. E. L. MASSIE, D.D.S., F.A.C.P.
SYRACUSE, NY
- Consulted and assisted for busy prosthodontic office, specialization in implanting.

July 1988 – December 1988
DENTAL ASSISTANT
DR. BEN KESICH, D.D.S.
BRENTWOOD, NY
- Chairside assisting for General Dentistry specialization in orthodontics.

January 1986 – June 1988
DENTAL CLAIMS PROCESSOR
PRUDENTIAL
LONG ISLAND, NY
- Inputed and paid all crown, bridge and orthodontic claims while working with two computer systems.

October 1983 – August 1985
DENTAL ASSISTANT
DR. JOHN STARKO, D.D.S.
- Performed all dental assisting duties. Dr. Starko and I graduated the same year, it was each of our first Dentistry experiences!

PERSONAL ADDITION

- Being a dynamic individual, I enjoy the energy and constant change of the dental field and feel I would be a strong asset to your environment.
- I work hard both mentally and physically and learn quickly. I work well on my own as well as part of a team, taking great pride in my work.
- I'm people-oriented, love life, and live it to its fullest, making the most of each day.
- My interests include walks with my dog, skiing, hiking, camping, the outdoors, cooking, crafts, spiritual retreats and playing guitar.

RELEVANT SKILLS AND EXPERIENCE

CHAIRSIDE ASSISTING

- Assisted dentists with procedures – x-rays, prophy and fluoride, placing rubber dams, while making sure procedures flowed smoothly from start to finish.
- Completed charting for new and repeat patients – charted required work, determined time required by dentist for procedure, and ensured medical history and all pertinent information was up to date.
- Developed a rapport with patients – explained procedures, calmed any fears, and showed a genuine interest in patient.
- Wrote estimates and obtained records for preauthorization – impressions, and intraoral photos
- Trained new staff and developed a procedures manual

STERILIZATION AND LABORATORY PROCEDURES

- Cleaned and sterilized all instruments and equipment using proper asepsis techniques.
- Organized procedure bins and trays making sure all instruments, burs, and cotton products were on trays
- Monitored inventory and ensured adequate supplies were available. Met with dental supply representatives to receive updates on new products and place orders.
- Poured and trimmed models, made custom trays, templates, occlusal rims and mouthguards.

RECEPTION

- Scheduled and confirmed appointments, booked referral appointments, and organized recall systems
- Responsible for Accounts Receivables – collections from patients and insurance companies.
- Input procedure codes and fees, new patient information and insurance information in computer.
- Created and sent insurance forms and preauthorizations.
- Updated computer with new fee guides and composed letters.

SPECIAL SKILLS

- Worked with prosthodontist in crown, bridge, denture and implant cases – used myomonitor and kinesiograph, created temporary crowns, assisted with implant procedures, organized timing of appointments between oral surgeon, periodontist and prosthodontist and ordered implant hardware.
- Assisted general dentist with orthodontic procedures – placed brackets and bands, checked appliances and discussed oral hygiene with patients.
- Assisted Dentists in creating and organizing two satellite offices (from blue printing, to ordering supplies, moving, and maintaining offices). Thoroughly enjoyed the endeavor, as it was challenging and exciting.

EDUCATION

CPR CERTIFICATION
July, 1992
ST. JOHN'S AMBULANCE
Long Island, NY

ORTHODONTIC ASSISTING CERTIFICATION
October 1984 – August 1985
INTERNATIONAL ASSOCIATION FOR ORTHODONTICS
New York, NY

PROPHYLAXIS AND FLUORIDE CERTIFICATION
August 1984
WEST SIDE INSTITUTE OF TECHNOLOGY
Received Honors:
New York, NY

REGISTERED DENTAL ASSISTING LEVEL II CERTIFICATION
August 1982 – June 1983
(Received certification with Intra Oral Skills. Honors in Practice Management)
Newark, NY

HIGH SCHOOL DIPLOMA
1975 – 1980
RIVER FRONT HIGH SCHOOL
(Received diploma as a Spanish Bilingual Student. Honors in Spanish, Drama and English)
Long Island, NY

Joanne Young (222) 555-7868

Resume Inside

Ross Schultz
123 Seaside Road
Vancouver, B.C.
V5R 1P3
(222) 555–8678

Energetic

Self Motivated

Hard working

HIGHLIGHTS OF QUALIFICATIONS

- Over 10 years experience in serving medical and research laboratory instruments.
- Dependable and reliable, can be counted on to get the job done.
- Learn new skills quickly.
- People oriented and get along well with others.

▲ **PERSONAL ADDITION**

You will find that I am a very sincere person. I enjoy working hard both mentally and physically. I work well on my own and as part of a team. I take pride in my work and take great satisfaction in a job well done.

I have a great sense of humor and am people oriented. Getting to know my customers is a part of the job I enjoy. I am always eager to learn more and improve my skills.

Ross Schultz
(222) 555–8678

▶ EDUCATION

Diploma of Technology in Electrical Technology and Instrumentation.

British Columbia Institute of Technology, 1982

High School Diploma
Frank Sr. High School
1980
Whistler, B.C.

Further Education

Programming in Fortran
Introduction to DOS
Programming in Basic
St. John's First Aid Course
WHMIS Course

INTERESTS

Hang gliding
Camping
Swimming
Golfing
Skiing
Racquet Sports
Travelling

▶ RELEVANT SKILLS AND EXPERIENCE

Technical

- Serviced clinical instruments and completed scheduled maintenance calls.
- Gave technical support over the telephone.
- Determined appropriate action to be taken: if the customer could independently solve the problem, if a service call was required, or if an instrument should be sent in.
- Sourced technical information through manuals and technical bulletins.
- Provided estimates for equipment repairs.

Organization

- Prioritized service calls.
- Scheduled work at customer's convenience.
- Monitored inventory and ensured adequate stock was available. Reordered parts when stock at minimum level.
- Coordinated service calls with maintenance calls.

Teamwork

- Created positive rapport with co-workers.
- Looked for sales opportunities for the company.
- Brainstormed ways to streamline the company's operations.
- Work equally well as a team leader and player.

Communication

- Calmed excited customers so they could give required information: nature of problem, urgency, and customer's ability to complete simple repairs on their own.
- Questioned customer to see if problem was hardware, software, or application oriented.
- Provided step by step problem-solving instructions over the telephone.

Ross Schultz
(222 555–8678)

▶ WORK EXPERIENCE

Sept. 1990
– Present
Senior Service Representative
Scientific Instruments, Hope, B.C.

- Serviced and maintained medical, research, and industrial instruments.

March 1984
– Sept. 1990
Technical Service Representative
Scientific Instruments, Hope, B.C.

- Maintained and serviced laboratory instruments.

May 1983
– June 1983
Operator/Laborer
Rockstone Inc., Whistler, B.C.

- Operated portable sawmill

Sept. 1983
– Jan. 1984
Carpenter Assistant

July 1983
– Sept. 1983
Fish Guide
Fishing Plus Whistler, B.C.

- Escorted guests on fishing tours.
- Maintained boats and engines.

June 1979
– Aug. 1979
Mechanic's Assistant
The Marina, Squamish, B.C.

- Repaired marine, chainsaw, and lawnmower engines.
- Installed throttle, gearshift and steering controls on boats.

Chapter 2

Cover Letters

ETA
30 min

Your cover letter is also an important component of your resume package.

Why?

As an introduction to you and your skills, a cover letter highlights your qualifications and determines whether an employer will continue on to your resume. Keep cover letters **short** and **interesting.** An employer faced with a pile of resumes often reads the shortest letters first.

Be sure to customize each cover letter to the position you are applying for. Do not use a form letter.

The Greeting

"The aim of learning is not knowledge but action."

Bits & Pieces, March 1990

Each cover letter should be addressed to a specific individual. If only the company's name is given in the advertisement, call to ask to whom you should address your letter. Be sure to inquire how the person prefers to be addressed and ask for the correct spelling of their name. It is surprising the impact this has on an employer and even more surprising how few people do it! This also gives you a contact name when you call to ask about the position.

 Unfortunately, this is impossible when responding to a box number.

Example:

From:	Dear Human Resource Manager,
	Dear Hiring Supervisor,
	Dear Sir/Madam,
	To Whom It May Concern,
To:	Dear Terry Jones,
	Dear Ms. Jones,
	Dear Ms. Terry Jones,

Opening Sentence

You must have a **dynamic opening sentence** to spark an employer's interest. Do not begin with, "I am submitting my resume in response to your ad in *The News* for the position of…"

 "Courage is simply the willingness to be afraid and act anyway."

Dr. Robert Anthony, *Think On*

Why?

The company is aware you are submitting a resume, they know where and when they advertised, and most of all, it says nothing about why you should be hired for the position.

A dynamic opening sentence describes your strongest attributes, how they relate to the job you are applying for, and why an employer should consider you.

Example:

1. "I am an accurate, efficient accountant dedicated to getting the job done."

2. "Proven ability to manage time, money, and people are my strong qualities."

3. "I take pride in being a fast and efficient cook who's food people come back for."

 List 15 things you are good at and 10 positive personal characteristics—you have at least this many! This will help give you ideas when creating your cover letters and personal addition. Review them periodically when you need a boost.

he Content

The content of the cover letter highlights the skills you have to offer. Determine what an employer values by:

- Speaking with the employer directly
- Interviewing employees with similar job duties
- Thoroughly reading the job advertisement

Make sure the layout and content of your cover letter is interesting or an employer may never get past it to see how unique your resume is!

Sometimes the employer asks for specifics such as:

- "familiarity with WordPerfect 5.1"

- "degree in Marketing or Business Administration"

Be sure to include this information in your cover letter.

The Sell

Read each completed cover letter out loud to yourself. Be sure it sounds interesting enough to catch and keep an employer's attention.

This section of your letter is composed of two elements:

- What **you** can offer a potential employer,

- Why you would like to work for the company,

    . . . all in one or two short sentences.

Example:

"I have extensive experience in the woodworking field and take pride in my dedication to quality craftsmanship and timely completion of projects. Your company's commitment to its customers is something I admire and value strongly."

# The Close

This final section includes:

- where you may be reached,
- when **you** will follow up.

 "It's a funny thing about life—if you refuse to accept anything but the best you often get it."

Somerset Maugham

Stating you will call the employer on a certain day not only shows initiative and interest in the position, it gives you a legitimate reason to call for an update on the competition. **Be sure** to call back when you stated you would.

Example:

1. "I look forward to the opportunity to further discuss my suitability for the woodworking position and will call you Monday, February 15. I may be also be reached at (123) 555–3333 should you have any questions."

2. "I know I would be a productive addition to your team and will call you on Wednesday, June 11, to answer any questions you may have. I may also be reached at (123) 555–4444."

For more examples of great cover letters, look for *Cover Letters Made Easy.*

Chapter 3

Job Applications

Even though submitting a resume is the standard method of applying for a job, some companies still ask you to fill out a job application. Even though most of the information they ask for will already be in your resume, you must fill one out anyway.

"He who controls others is powerful, but he who has mastered himself is mightier still."

Lao–tzu

How?

- If possible, take the application home with you and type out your answers. When it is completed, **hand deliver** it!

Pick up a job application from a government office or large corporation and practice completing it. This gives you time to decide how to respond and a completed form to refer to in future.

- If you cannot type your responses, **print** legibly so that it is easy to read.

- Use **pen** rather than pencil—it is easier to read.

- Answer everything on the application, giving as much information as possible.

- Refer to your resume to be sure your dates and titles are accurate.

- If there is a section asking if there is any other information you wish them to know, be sure to fill it out! Think of it as your personal addition. It will give you an opportunity to tell them all the reasons you would be an excellent candidate for the position.

- An application form will often ask if you have any health concerns that would affect your job performance. Do not be offended. Presumably you would not apply for a position you are not physically capable of doing.

- Attach a copy of your resume to the application.

"You can often change things if you just change your attitude."

Bits & Pieces, October 1992

Do not think of the job application as an inconvenience. Instead, think of it as a great opportunity to round out your resume and answer specific employer questions. It is simply another step in the process. Do it **neatly, thoroughly** and **professionally** and it **will** pay off!

Chapter 4

Other Marketing Ideas

You may decide to create personalized marketing tools to remind employers of who you are and what you have to offer. The more familiar an employer is with your name, the greater the chance you will be remembered!

Sales Brochures

Marketing tools may be used as introduction or follow-up aids.

Highlight strong points you want employers to remember and add a personal touch to your brochure. Give brochures to employers and friends. You never know when a friend will pass one on to a prospective employer.

Business Cards

Anyone can have a business card printed up, so why don't you? Design yours to reflect your skills and personal style. Give them to people you meet at networking functions and to everyone else you know. A business card is an inexpensive and unique marketing tool you can carry everywhere you go.

Chapter 5

The Next Stages

You have your marketing tools. Now what do you do with them? The key to securing employment lies in how and where you look.

Networking

Although networking, which involves meeting the right people, seems to be the hardest thing to learn and do during your job search, it is certainly the most important component. How can you expect to find a job quickly if no one knows you are looking?

It is certainly who you know as much as what you know that gets you a job. Get out and meet people, you will eventually meet someone who helps you get work.

If you are new to the job hunt, start slowly, but start! It is all too easy to simply look in the paper each week for jobs you feel you would be suited for and convince yourself you are effectively looking for work. Unfortunately it will be a long and frustrating process with very few rewards. With 200 and 300 applications being submitted for advertised positions, you need to land a job before it is advertised!

Trust us...Start chatting today with people you know about the type of work you are seeking. People are more than willing to help and, who knows, maybe the next time you chat it will be them looking for a new job.

ob Interviews

Now that you have begun to deliver your resumes to employers, be patient. Eventually you will be called for interviews.

The key to successful interviews is in the preparation. You guessed it, the interview process has changed as much as the resume has. Do not be caught off guard. Instead, show employers your interview skills are as up–to–date as your resume.

 "The only thing that can stop any one of us from learning new behaviors is ourselves."
Ernie Zelinski

Join us in *Job Interviews Made Easy,* where we let you in on the latest techniques for a knock 'em dead interview.

That Was Then...

- A resume was a litany of everything you have ever done—no matter how many pages it took.

- You put a "job objective" on your resume.

- You included your Social Security Number and other personal information on your resume.

- You included your last salary and reason for leaving on your resume.

- You included a cover sheet with only your name on it with your resume.

- You enclosed your resume in a clear plastic folder.

- Hand-written resumes and cover letters were acceptable.

- You never called an employer for feedback.

- It was embarrassing to be unemployed, so you never told anyone.

- Five or ten applications for a position was normal, and resumes were often not even necessary.

- You rarely took credit for your accomplishments, let alone pat yourself on the back for them.

- You mailed your resume rather delivering it in person.

- You often had one or two job offers within a week.

- If you were hired by a big company, you often worked there until retirement.

This Is Now...

- Your resume is a personalized and dynamic two or three page advertisement of your skills and qualifications.

- Your resume is done on a computer and laser printer.

- You do not limit your opportunities by including a job objective on your resume.

- You do not put personal information on your resume.

- Employers often receive 200 to 300 applications for each position.

- A great resume is a must!

- You take credit for all your accomplishments and include them in your resume.

- Landing one interview for every 10 resume submissions is excellent.

- You submit your resume by hand.

- No job is forever.

Conclusion

Now you are prepared to go out and knock 'em dead. Your resume looks professional and is a dynamic reflection of what you have to offer an employer. You know how to write an eye–catching and effective cover letter, and you have all your supplementary marketing tools prepared.

"You're never a loser until you quit trying."

Mike Ditka

Remember, looking for work is a full time job. Surround yourself with positive people and try not to get discouraged. If you need to take a day off once in a while to re–energize then do so. But remember, the perfect career is not going to come without some hard work on your part. Keep your resume current, customizing it as often as possible.

Persevere and you will be successful. Once you begin meeting and networking with people you may be surprised at the unique and challenging opportunities that will present themselves. The job market is changing but by no means is it dying. Be creative and positive in your job search and you will succeed.

Now that you have a winning resume, the next stages will certainly be the job hunt and interview. Just like resumes these processes have changed considerably over the years. See you in *Job Hunting Made Easy* and *Job Interviews Made Easy!*

VGM CAREER BOOKS

CAREER DIRECTORIES
Careers Encyclopedia
Dictionary of Occupational
 Titles
Occupational Outlook
 Handbook

CAREERS FOR
Animal Lovers
Bookworms
Computer Buffs
Crafty People
Culture Lovers
Environmental Types
Film Buffs
Foreign Language Aficionados
Good Samaritans
Gourmets
History Buffs
Kids at Heart
Nature Lovers
Night Owls
Number Crunchers
Plant Lovers
Shutterbugs
Sports Nuts
Travel Buffs

CAREERS IN
Accounting; Advertising;
Business; Child Care;
Communications; Computers;
Education; Engineering;
the Environment; Finance;
Government; Health Care;
High Tech; Journalism; Law;
Marketing; Medicine;
Science; Social &
Rehabilitation Services

CAREER PLANNING
Admissions Guide to Selective
 Business Schools
Beating Job Burnout
Beginning Entrepreneur
Career Planning &
 Development for College
 Students & Recent Graduates
Career Change

Careers Checklists
Cover Letters They Don't
 Forget
Executive Job Search Strategies
Guide to Basic Cover Letter
 Writing
Guide to Basic Resume Writing
Guide to Temporary
 Employment
Job Interviews Made Easy
Joyce Lain Kennedy's Career
 Book
Out of Uniform
Resumes Made Easy
Slam Dunk Resumes
Successful Interviewing for
 College Seniors
Time for a Change

CAREER PORTRAITS
Animals   Nursing
Cars   Sports
Computers   Teaching
Music   Travel

GREAT JOBS FOR
Communications Majors
English Majors
Foreign Language Majors
History Majors
Psychology Majors

HOW TO
Approach an Advertising
 Agency and Walk Away with
 the Job You Want
Bounce Back Quickly After
 Losing Your Job
Choose the Right Career
Find Your New Career Upon
 Retirement
Get & Keep Your First Job
Get Hired Today
Get into the Right Business
 School
Get into the Right Law School
Get People to Do Things Your
 Way
Have a Winning Job Interview

Hit the Ground Running in
 Your New Job
Improve Your Study Skills
Jump Start a Stalled Career
Land a Better Job
Launch Your Career in TV
 News
Make the Right Career Moves
Market Your College Degree
Move from College into a
 Secure Job
Negotiate the Raise You
 Deserve
Prepare a Curriculum Vitae
Prepare for College
Run Your Own Home Business
Succeed in College
Succeed in High School
Write a Winning Resume
Write Successful Cover Letters
Write Term Papers & Reports
Write Your College Application
 Essay

OPPORTUNITIES IN
This extensive series provides
detailed information on nearly
150 individual career fields.

RESUMES FOR
Advertising Careers
Banking and Financial Careers
Business Management Careers
College Students &
 Recent Graduates
Communications Careers
Education Careers
Engineering Careers
Environmental Careers
50 + Job Hunters
Health and Medical Careers
High School Graduates
High Tech Careers
Law Careers
Midcareer Job Changes
Sales and Marketing Careers
Scientific and Technical Careers
Social Service Careers
The First-Time Job Hunter

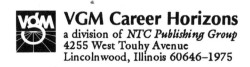
VGM Career Horizons
a division of *NTC Publishing Group*
4255 West Touhy Avenue
Lincolnwood, Illinois 60646–1975